My Parents Taught Me My Good Manners

Teaching Manners and Etiquette to Kids

by The Sincere Seeker Kids Collection

HELLO

SMILE

My parents taught me to greet others and to smile; it's a kind gesture!

My parents taught me to be good to others and treat everyone the way I want to be treated.

My parents taught me to always be kind to animals.

My parents taught me to always obey and help my parents.

My parents taught me to forgive others and not hold grudges.

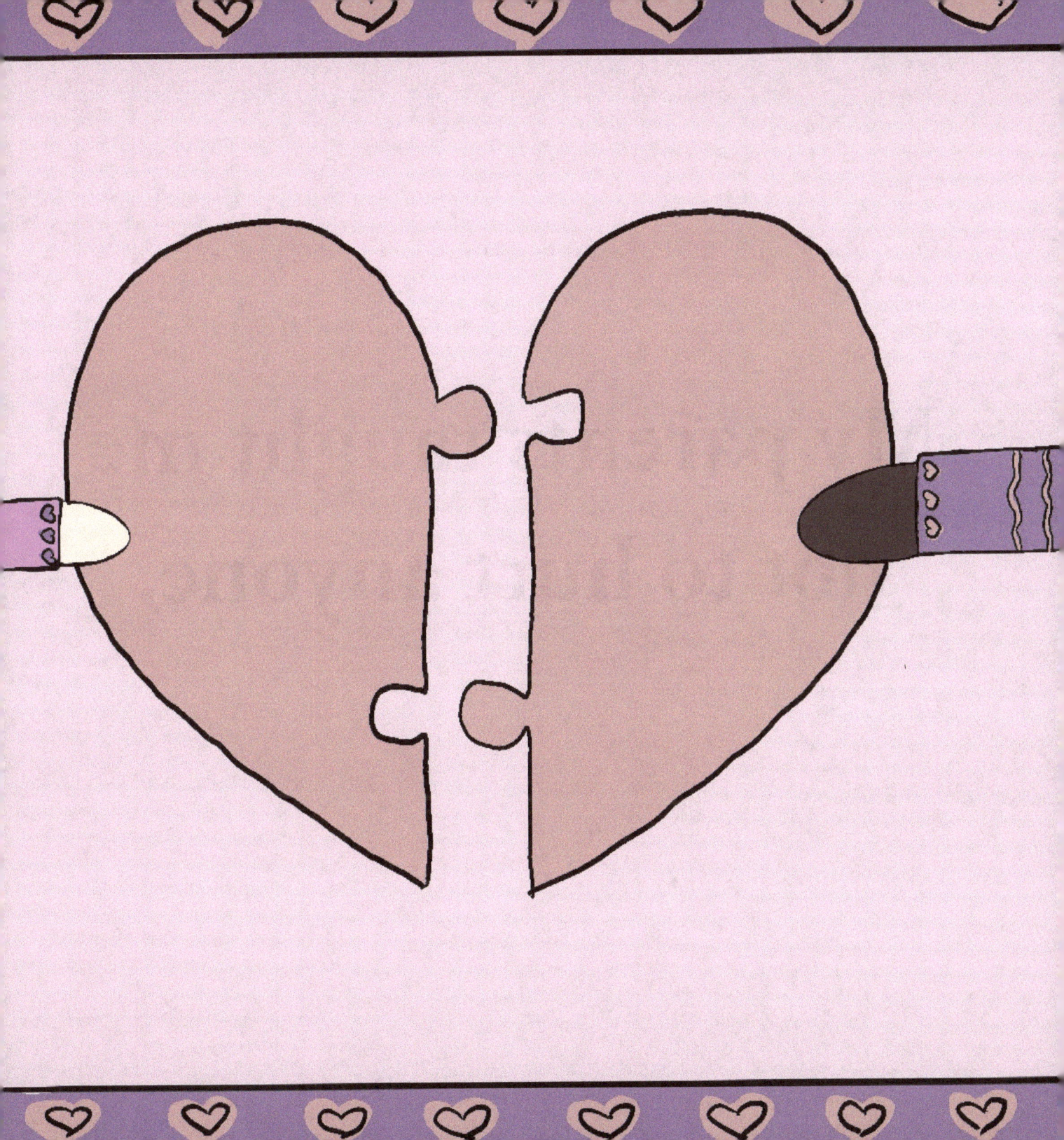

My parents taught me
not to hurt anyone.

My parents taught me not to lose my cool and get angry!

My parents taught me to eat slowly with my mouth closed and not to talk while I eat.

My parents taught me to cover my mouth and nose when I sneeze with a tissue. If I don't have one, I will cover my nose and mouth with my elbow and not my hands. Then I will throw the tissue in the garbage and wash my hands with soap.

My parents taught me to give to others, especially those in need.

My parents taught me to be patient.

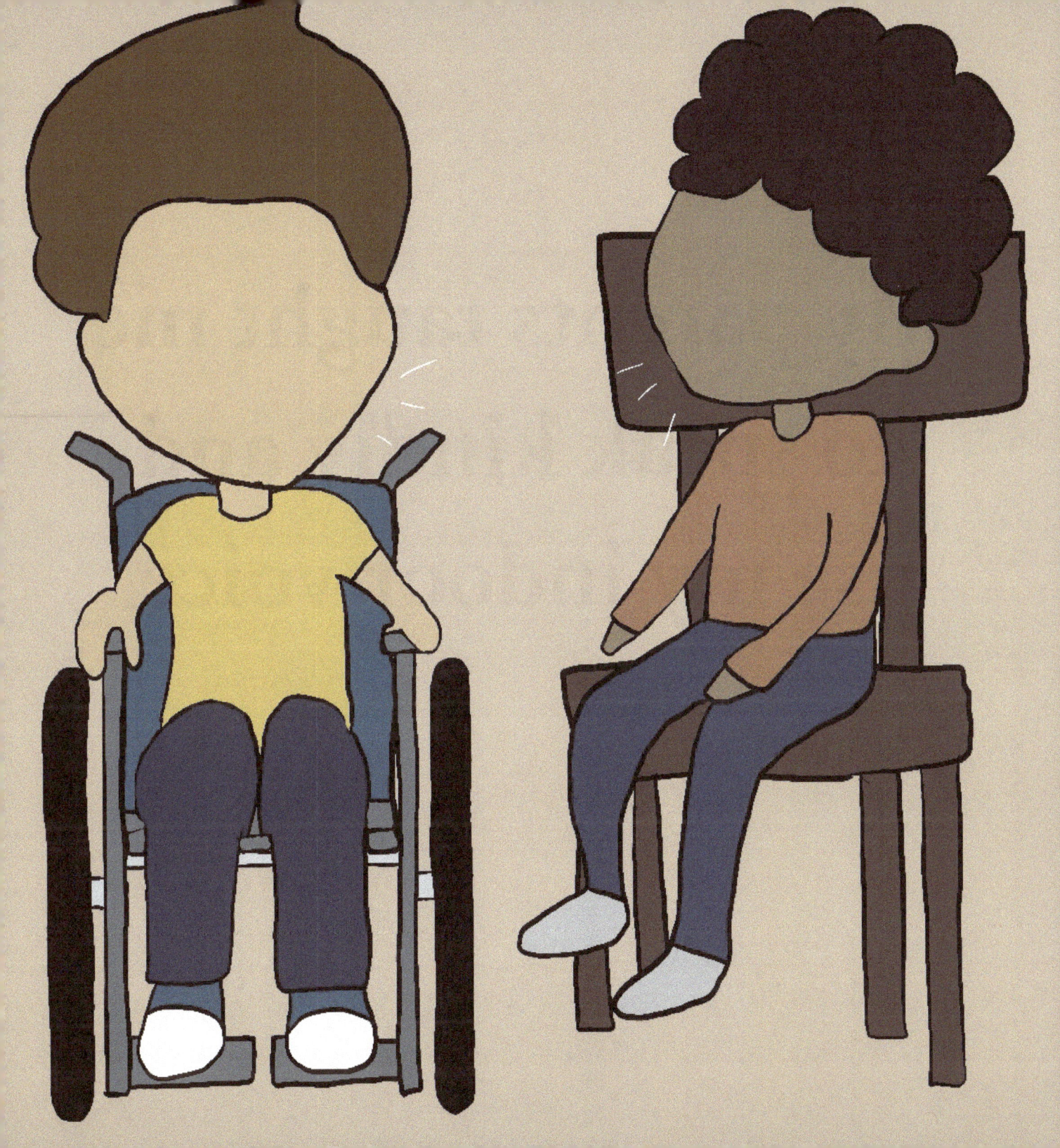

My parents taught me to speak kindly and use my indoor voice.

My parents taught me to keep my promises and not break them!

MY MAMA MADE
PIZZA FOR US

My parents taught me to honor my guests and offer them food and drinks!

My parents taught me to always remember God, and He will remember me!

My parents taught me never to cheat, whether it's cheating on my homework or when I'm playing a board game with my family and friends.

My parents taught me to always be honest and never lie.

My parents taught me to say *please* when asking for something– it's polite to say please!

My parents taught me to always be grateful, thank God for everything, and thank those who helped me.

My parents taught me to wash my hands after using the bathroom, clip my fingernails and toenails, and brush my teeth.

My parents taught me that God loves me and that I should love Him too!

My parents taught me to share some of what I have with others because sharing is caring!

My parents taught me to always do my homework and read many books to gain more knowledge!

The End.

www.ingramcontent.com/pod-product-compliance
Lightning Source LLC
Chambersburg PA
CBHW081307140626
46546CB00022B/3444